Let's Talk About
BEING SELFISH

Let's Talk About
BEING SELFISH

By JOY BERRY

Illustrated by John Costanza
Edited by Orly Kelly
Designed by Jill Losson

GROLIER ENTERPRISES CORP.

Let's talk about BEING SELFISH.

Have you ever been with a person who was eating something and would not share it with you?

Have you ever played with a person who would not share his or her toys with you?

People who do not share their things with others are SELFISH.

SELFISH people care only about themselves. They do not care about the thoughts and feelings of other people.

When you are with someone who is selfish —
- how do you feel?
- what do you think?
- what do you do?

When you are with someone who is selfish —

- you may feel left out, frustrated and angry;
- you may think, "This person is not fun to be with";
- you may choose not to play with the person.

It is important to treat other people the way you want to be treated.

If you want people to share their things with you, you will need to share your things with them.

You will need to be unselfish.

Being unselfish does not mean that you have to share all of your things all of the time.

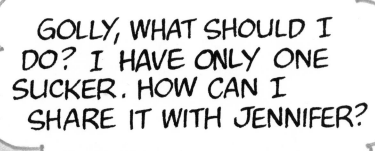

If you have something to eat and
there is not enough to share with
the person you are with, put
the food away.

Try not to eat food in front of a person
who does not have anything to eat.

If you are going to share some food or anything else with another person, try to be as fair as possible.

Here is a good rule to follow when you are dividing something:

- Let one person do the dividing and the other person do the choosing.

If you have something special that you do not want to share, do not use it in front of another person.

That is, unless —

- the other person is content not to use it, or
- the other person has something else to use.

You do not have to share your things with anyone who may lose or damage them.

Put your things away if you are afraid this might happen.

When you share your things, help the other person take care of them.

- Show the person how to use your things in the right way.
- Tell the person where to use your things.

If there is only one thing that must be shared by two or more people, be fair.

- Take turns using it.
- Let each person use it for an equal amount of time. Someone can count, or you can use a clock or timer to help keep track of the time.

If you want to be happy, you will treat other people the way you want to be treated.

This means you will not be selfish because you do not want other people around you to be selfish.